BUZZKILL CLAMSHELL

ADVANCE PRAISE FOR *BUZZKILL CLAMSHELL*

"'Pain is a match,' opens *Buzzkill Clamshell*, and so is this collection: both a hot, bright, sudden flare in the dark and a swipe right, an immense YES of delicious recognition. Unafraid to keen keenly for what's unfinished, wounded, shuttered, Amber Dawn's poetry knows that being a buzzkill is a world-making process: mythically vivid and skinless in its witchy vitality that spells and sings exactly the heart of what poetry is."
—SO MAYER, author of *Truth & Dare*

"I never quite know what I'm going to experience with Amber Dawn's poetry, but I do know I'll get a bit of new sexy language mixed in with some body heat! *Buzzkill Clamshell* does this with added layers of body horror, body honour, and a little bit of lesbian prayer. Ablaze with poetic dexterity, *Buzzkill Clamshell* is plush with a lesbian gaze that focuses in on desire, pelvic girdles, body fluids, and an ugly attraction to one's self. Amber Dawn offers us a sarcastic but compassionate view of ourselves."
—SHARANPAL RUPRAI, author of *Seva* and *Pressure Cooker Love Bomb*

"Hold on to your hearts, readers! Queer lit's favourite fierce femme and force of nature Amber Dawn is back, and she's taking no prisoners. Ribald and unrepentant, in turns ferocious and tender, the poems in *Buzzkill Clamshell* showcase the author's trademark wit and emotional range as they map the terrain of sexuality, aging, chronic illness, and trauma with gorgeous language that is somehow both shocking and subtle. Amber Dawn masterfully reinterprets lyrical and confessional poetic forms, effortlessly weaving motifs drawn from history, mythology, religion, pop culture, and autobiography to illustrate the profound in the profane, and vice versa. Resilience has never looked quite so sexy or so sacred."
—KAI CHENG THOM, author of *Falling Back in Love With Being Human*

"In an exquisite act of agency, these poems approach chronic pain as collaborator, crafting an erotics of chronic pain that is both raunchy and surprisingly tender. Rooted in the tradition of horror as queer playscape for transgressive possibilities, this is a world where 'to be monstrous is perverse medicine.' Under the hot filth, the abjection, the camp, the horror, the mythmaking, and the thrilling visceral ride of its inventive language, this book has a thread of devotion, where devotion is staying with something as it is, desiring to know it deeply enough to be transformed. Carmen Maria Machado's queer horror meets Audre Lorde's erotics in a filthy bathroom stall, written as only Amber Dawn ever could."
—ANNA SWANSON, author of *The Garbage Poems*

BUZZKILL CLAMSHELL

Poems

Amber Dawn

ARSENAL PULP PRESS
VANCOUVER

ARSENAL PULP PRESS
Suite 202 – 211 East Georgia St.
Vancouver, BC V6A 1Z6
Canada
arsenalpulp.com

The publisher gratefully acknowledges the support of the Canada Council for the Arts and the British Columbia Arts Council for its publishing program and the Government of Canada and the Government of British Columbia (through the Book Publishing Tax Credit Program) for its publishing activities.

British Columbia | British Columbia Arts Council An agency of the Province of British Columbia | Canada Council for the Arts Conseil des arts du Canada | Canada

Arsenal Pulp Press acknowledges the xʷməθkʷəy̓əm (Musqueam), Sḵwx̱wú7mesh (Squamish), and səlilwətaɬ (Tsleil-Waututh) Nations, custodians of the traditional, ancestral, and unceded territories where our office is located. We pay respect to their histories, traditions, and continuous living cultures and commit to accountability, respectful relations, and friendship.

Cover design by Rebecca Poulin in collaboration with Jazmin Welch
Cover art by Rebecca Chaperon, *Moon Pearls*
Author photo by Amber Dawn
Text design by Jazmin Welch
Edited by Dina Del Bucchia
Copy-edited by Catharine Chen
Proofread by Alison Strobel

Printed and bound in Canada

Library and Archives Canada Cataloguing in Publication:
Title: Buzzkill clamshell : poems / Amber Dawn.
Names: Amber Dawn, 1974– author.
Identifiers: Canadiana (print) 20240434889 | Canadiana (ebook) 20240434900 | ISBN 9781551529790 (softcover) | ISBN 9781551529806 (EPUB)
Subjects: LCGFT: Poetry.
Classification: LCC PS8607.A9598 B89 2025 | DDC C811/.6—dc23

ACKNOWLEDGMENTS

Buzzkill Clamshell was brought to life with support—creatively, emotionally, and sometimes bodily—from many weird geniuses. Deeply felt thank yous:

to Rebecca Chaperon for the hauntingly beautiful artwork;

to Dina Del Bucchia for being a patient, wise, and hilarious editor;

to the team at Arsenal Pulp Press for taking yet another risk on my work—Brian Lam, Catharine Chen, JC Cham, Jazmin Welch, Rebecca Poulin, Cynara Geissler, and Robert Ballantyne;

to my Quad Writing Group—Megan Milks, Dia Felix, and Adèle Barclay;

to my Object writing collaborators—Vi Khi Nao and Jessica Alexander;

to Michelle Tea for her Writing for Witches workshop;

to Anna Camilleri and Wy Joung Kou for their HELD: Writing Disability Futures Workshop;

to the literary magazines that uplifted several of these poems through publication—*Plenitude Magazine*, *Stone of Madness*

Press, *Venus Magazine*, *Eavesdrop Magazine*, *The Ampersand Review*, *manywor(l)ds*, and *Pink Disco*;

to my early readers and their kind words—So Mayer, Eli Tareq El Bechelany-Lynch, Anna Swanson, Kai Cheng Thom, Sharanpal Ruprai, and Arielle Greenberg;

and to the many loves who cared for me and talked with me about pain—CJ Rowe, Farah Khan, Amanda Lamarche, Zena Sharman, Justin Ducharme, Anoushka Ratnarajah, Brie Grey-Noble, Jillian Christmas, and Maya Suess.

Writing about pain only brings more pain, throwing me out of that sweet disassociation I live every day. Am I sacrificing my joints to be a poet?

—ELI TAREQ EL BECHELANY-LYNCH, *knot body*

This is a difficult story to tell,
not because it was like a fairy tale
but because it was not.

—SO MAYER, "what do you do with a curse"

CONTENTS

13 The Erotics of Chronic Pain
15 The Erotics of Chronic Pain #2
17 Age Play
19 Intraoperative Photographs
24 depersonalization is an altered state of identity
26 Aubrey Beardsley: *The Burial of Salomé*, 1893
30 Francesco del Cossa: *Santa Lucia of Syracuse*, 1472
33 Cunnus Renatus
35 Bedrest
39 The Erotics of Chronic Pain #3
40 Unnamed Service Road
45 Safe Space: A Monosyllabic Rewrite of Ann Cvetkovich's *An Archive of Feelings*
47 Pink Disco
49 Woe to the max.
52 Unfinished Poem
56 Selkie
57 Swan Maiden
58 Lewis Carroll Could Never

59 Janara
61 Canidia
64 Henry Fuseli: *Titania and Bottom*, 1790
68 Hostile Architecture
71 YOUR PARTICIPATION IS VOLUNTARY
76 IT
77 PINHEAD
79 SKEKSIS
81 XENOMORPH
88 depersonalization is an altered state of identity #2
89 Medications that cause hair loss:
93 Chilly Down
96 The *Twin Peaks* Theme Song
100 Cosmological Touch
101 Our swollen tongues brunch in the underworld.
103 Stable in the Sky
110 depersonalization is an altered state of identity #3
112 Buzzkill Clamshell ISO Goddamn
113 Lez Prophéties

The Erotics of Chronic Pain

I can rid myself of an aching back by turning
somersaults to the rhythm of a whippoorwill's call.

This quagmiry body never rests in a cut grass nest.
Set to roost in a rotten log, decay is my camouflage.

My lover is a necrotroph. How sweetly she eats my bloat. Cum
foams from my nose. I will gift her a tooth if she stays until spring.

When people mimicry my language, they say "whip or will."
But the direct translation is "pain is coming" "pain is coming."

Pain is a match. My femur is hot ember—calcium becomes ash
and ash and ash. I don't know a phoenix from nothing.

Fire finds my throat. Each sound I make is raked coal.
An orgasm coated in soot. My lover chokes on the smoke.

If I cut out the heart of a sparrow and hold it under
my tongue, then I will understand the language of birds.

When I am ready to meet darkness, I will follow a whippoorwill's call.
If a whippoorwill flies into my kitchen, I'll warm my last bowl of soup.

This leached marsh body of mine was never meant
to resurrect, still, how sweetly my lover builds a nest.

The Erotics of Chronic Pain #2

This pain is a poisoned snag. An old saw does what an old saw does
what an old saw. I'll never write the word *trauma* in a poem again.

Canker girdles branch after branch and my lover has the patience
of a ripping blade greased in beeswax. I would submit to her,

but my pelvic floor already belongs to rot—sugar and cellulose,
swollen and spongy. And I need something stronger than analgesics.

She is aces with anything made of metal. She cuts the gusset
from my post-op underwear with one deft hand. My labium

shivers against the steel heel. What forms in the cleft between
past █████ and present pain is called woundwood. Widespread

dieback, discoloured callus, and still she has the faith of a falling
axe. Why can't change be as graceful as the volta in a poem?

Time is a fallacy and yet the light shifts from golden to blue
and we are still in the woods. Time is a fallacy and yet I feel

my sacrum slowly being eaten alive. I want her to love me like termites
love a nurse log. I want her like a felled tree wants to turn back into soil.

There is no wrong way to read *Carmilla.*
If a vampire bite is to be viewed
as a repossession
of the queer body, then view it as such.

Age Play

I am a pill bottle trying to catch her fist.
Percocet is also pink and round.

Pink and round like the rims of her childhood bicycle.
I swallow her greased front tire first, then the back.
Can recovered memory be unrecovered? Can gape
be ungaped? A miscalculation of glut. Forget
cunt busting, nostalgia play is the edge. Extreme longing.
I'll shit Spokey Dokeys and handlebar tassels tomorrow.
Huffy Dream Girl never safewords.

She is kind and reminds me that a drained
swimming pool is still aqua blue. That's aftercare.

She is cruel and fine strands of my hair
are caught in the prongs of her tourmaline ring.

I have the emotional capacity of a lone moth shivering under a street lamp.
But physically, I am as plastic as a lawn ornament flamingo. Mentally,
I am a warm body being fucked on the neighbour's fresh cut lawn.

I want to be as exotic as Florida and we're making new memories.
I want to be a scoop of cherry ice cream fallen from its cone.
Good puddle. Sweet melt. Ruined pink is a colour.

Pain scale red is a colour. I'm a ten, but
my medication causes memory loss.

My lover is boo boo, babycake, li'l bit. Again with peeling
back the years. She smears valentine hearts on the vanity mirror.
And happy faces. And stickmen. Daisies. The sun. But in this scene,
she refuses to let me be her reflection. Never ever a baby double.
Never toddler twin. I am the fluted aluminium lipstick case
without its tube of rouge. Altogether spent.
In this scene, I am a gouged out cylinder.

Intraoperative Photographs

I saw a flamboyance
of flamingos once, in a zoo
in Orlando, Florida.

I saw a man go over Niagara Falls in a pickle barrel. He survived!
But he was immediately arrested and fined five hundred dollars for illegal
daredevilling in a public park. Only weeks later, he had an audience
laughing like rats as a guest on the *Tonight Show* and was voted one
of the "10 Sexiest Men in the World" by *Mademoiselle* magazine.
He feathered his hair like the drummer in Mötley Crüe. This was the 1980s.

I saw an ex-boyfriend
light his fart on fire at a party.
Adolescence was a strange time.

I saw the famous mammoth of the castle—a one-million-year-old fossilized
pachyderm on display in a Renaissance palace in L'Aquila, Italy. I learned
that the castle was not a castle at all, but a fort built by Spanish invaders,
who forced the Aquilans to surrender their wool and saffron and melt all
the city's bells to make cannonballs. Those bell deprived Aquilans might be
my ancestors, who knows? Only one mammoth tusk was found and reunited
with the skull, which I thought made it something of a unicorn. But a tusk is not
a horn, it's a tooth. I saw a wicked big tooth. Archaeological science is something.

I saw an evangelical church
burn down to the slab
in Sherkston, Ontario.

I saw three-time Pulitzer Prize winner Edward Albee tell an audience of about five hundred of us, "I happen to be gay, but I am not a gay writer." The theatre seats were red velvet. Albee wore a blazer cut leather jacket. So, yeah, that adage about meeting your heroes—I had studied *Who's Afraid of Virginia Woolf?* in Introduction to Drama at college. Albee was a queer hero, yeah, on a queer stage accepting a queer lifetime achievement award. "I hope I am able to transcend my personal preferences," he said. The next day every gay was ticked off, especially on Twitter.

I saw the Spice Girls
on their Spiceworld Tour.
Baby wore a shirt that said Baby.

I saw Olympia Dukakis in the ladies' washroom at the NYU Skirball. Absurdly, I wanted her to recite the iconic line from *Steel Magnolias*: "The only thing that separates us from the animals is our ability to accessorize." That film might be my root. All those ostentatious Sunday hats, the over-the-top shouting and arm waving. Everybody thinks Daryl Hannah and Dolly were the Magnolia hotties. For me, it's Olympia. I'm all in with Olympia. I told her that she looked absolutely gorgeous before refreshing my fuchsia pink lipstick in the vanity mirror.

I saw a bat go for a swim
in the Rideau Canal during the daytime.
It was probably a bad omen.

I saw you in a series of intraoperative photographs sent from my surgeon's office by email. The reds and pinks of you I had expected, but not yellow. Sick yolk sac yellow. Self-aggrandizing yellow. Or mucus or rancid milk. Conditional stimulus yellow. Abnormalized cells yellow. Yellow now, and perhaps forever, associated with pain. How did my body hold your horror? You grew golf ball, then pomegranate, then double fist sized inside me. You had me walking funny the next day. Except every single day was the next day. You made pain my insignia. Firebrand on my hide. Or pockmark or blot. All my fantasies, my kinks, my private whims remade by pain. You turned my cunt into an empty endocarp, a buzzkill clamshell, a chuff trench or a cancer, a bent violence that even I can't describe in a poem.

At least my cunt
and her cunt
have mutual respect
for each other's sadness.

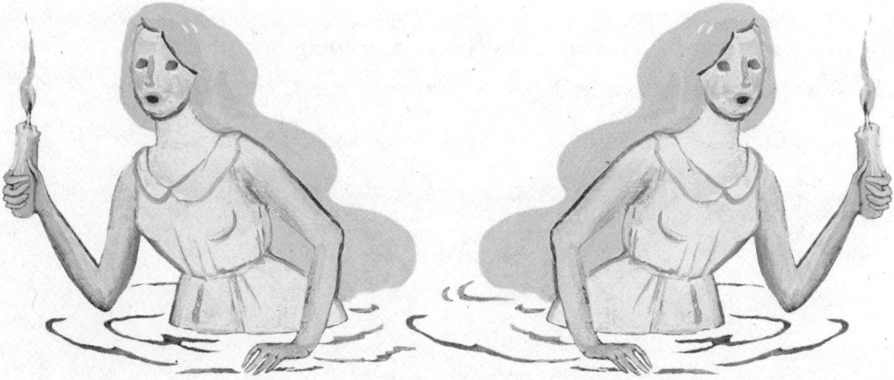

depersonalization is an altered state of identity

Raindrops spit the windshield. I am an August storm at 2 a.m.
And road grime and oil sheen and badly patched potholes.

I am the luminous trap of an opossum's eyes. I am meadowsweet
teasing the headlights, my tufted florets slow dance in the ditch.

I am slick flickering light spilling from the hazards. I am the pair of white
moths that fly in through the open window to circle the domed cabin light.

The nausea gurgling in the driver's throat. I am the smell of icky
peaches. I am the upset quart basket from the roadside farm stand.

One peach rests on the brown vinyl seat like a sleeping
baby. One peach is wedged in the dashboard crevice.

One peach is fresh mash under the driver's boot. I am the peach
cupped in the still hands of the passenger, wondrously unspoiled.

I am a nearly inaudible question, "What was that?"
And another question, "Did we hit something?"

I am Route 32 through the Drowned Lands flood plain.
I am the adrenalin that outsmarts oncoming whiplash pain.

I am blood pressure bowing out. And cortisol
And norepinephrine and vagal arousal.

People ask me "Are you all right?" and "Are you
in pain?" and "What happened to you?"

Survivors of sexual █████ are five times more prone to pelvic pain, loss
of mobility and excessive bleeding. But I just tell them it was a car crash.

Aubrey Beardsley

The Burial of Salomé, 1893

Moon gone Wilde. Drunken slip from the tableau. Finespun clothes
drifting in celestial blue. Maybe the moon is cruising a new paramour?

Maybe the moon is just new? An invisible blot on white paper. Peripheral
wan. But why describe what is far gone? What we can see is Salomé.

Dead centre, a focal and fuck-sized subject. The last and smallest version
of our heroine in Beardsley's sixteen decadent illustrations. No imposing

black robe, no tickling peacock feathers. An undraped take. Only one image
ago, she swung Jokanaan's severed head like game. Her aroused soliloquy—

I will kiss. I will bite. Thou art dead and thy head belongs to me. Femdom sermon,
flogging man's existential panic. One image ago, but why describe what is gone?

Now her cadaver is a silicone doll, limp as Victorian ideals, limp as christ
in la pietà. Cul-de-lampe. Bend me low, I might like breathless Salomé best.

Beardsley said, "If I am not grotesque, I am nothing." wowʍoʍ same.
When I am not grotesque, I feel the full dysphoric heft of chronic pain.

I want in on his indecency. Slip me into his lewd phantasmagoria.
I want my own sick cunt to be satirized in Beardsley's black ink.

I want to escape into Salomé's unbothered necrocunnus. I want to out-
bid the forbidden, out-blast the blasphemous. Now a masked dagger

and a smirking satyr carry her to a powder case coffin. Notice the parabolic twist of the satyr's arms, hands between her legs like our vanishing moon.

Prosaically viewed, this is a defilement of the body. I choose to see it as service. Figa wank funeral rites. Edification through cold orgasm.

Salomé's soul yanked to Elysium. PetitMorte4PetiteMorte.
A regal queening of our princess before she is laid to rest.

Lazing isn't lazing.
Nothing isn't nothing. Learn
the placid craft of time travel
while napping on velvet.

Francesco del Cossa

Santa Lucia of Syracuse, 1472

What seems clear enough: in 304 AD Lucy was tortured and put to death ... thus martyred for her Christianity. What is unclear: why, exactly, she runs around Gothic and Renaissance paintings holding a golden dish with her blue eyes staring weirdly out from it.
—MAGGIE NELSON, *Bluets*

How should I say it? Flora oculus? Optic glory?
Twin blooms on a tender stem. Not shimmer roses,
though. Not orchids. Unbodied eyes! Transposed
and growing like spring buds. In other portraits,

Santa Lucia's iconographic eyes are displayed
on a pewter dish, glass platter or chalice. Wait,
wait, I'll catch you up. Catholics masturbate
to punishment, violent torture, really, interpret

that how you will. It's all about mortified flesh,
you know, hot flagellation and hot slaughter, hot
severed body parts, suffering virgins off the charts,
but most of all, redemptive suffering—to embrace
mystical rebirth is the real cock fodder. I'm not
ready to admit that I prayed to the martyred saint

as I feared my own genital necrosis. If her gouged
out eyes could resurrect, then why not my cunt?
Anyway, del Cossa's painted altarpiece is different
in that she is not serving her eyes like amuse-bouches.

Instead, del Cossa rendered her eyes as a single stem
bouquet delicately held in trinity fingers—her thumb,
middle and pointer. Her body is whole and unharmed.
Robed in Renaissance finery, red ribbon, lace, almost

sensually draped as she kneels in gilded air. Vogue
gold and stable tempera, not cracking oil. And wood,
not canvas—she will last forever, she has withstood
two millennia already. Surviving your murderers must
be flush. To endure beyond the empire is poetry,
it's a lavish axe. So, yes, I prayed during recovery,

especially for my cunt, and there are many prayers
to Santa Lucia ready for me to recite, but I realized
that what I actually venerate is del Cossa's altarpiece.
His Santa Lucia's flowering eyes are not only healed,

they're a hybrid phenomenon, a doubling, a holy both.
To come back from persecution as something queerer,
miracle of miracles, a sacred thing, our shared cure.
How queer will my cunt become when the pain is gone?

Cunnus Renatus

My cunt is a musical snuffbox with a wind-up key
and ninety-six brass teeth tuned along a grinning comb.
When she cranks me in tight circles, I sing a sea shanty.
Speech is still new to me, so I only sing the simplest
of airs. Haul-one. Haul-two. Haul-belay. Bail out.
Stamp and go. Stormalong. Stormalong. Heave ho.
Fire down below. Way-ay-ya. Quid. Quid. Quim. Me.

My cunt is a fixed address and she is a pounce of feral cats.
Rough tongue. Rogue tongue. Rough tongue. Rouge tongue.
At last, I am as clean as a saucer of cream left out overnight.

My cunt is a gala apple picked in September and her bite
marks are logograms that tell my story. By late summer,
the nights had already turned cool. My petals fell. Fat dew
flecked the orchard before dawn. The air smelled like cider
and honey. Mason bees stayed all day. For her, I ripened.

My cunt is a churn hole carved into a limestone grotto
and she is a pilgrimager seeking cure. Miraculous swirl.
A sacred plunge pool, but only if she can hold her breath
and repeat "thy will be done" twelve times in her mind before
resurfacing again. Faith might be our only refuge from suffering.

She is a hair worker gumming a dead girl's curls into gold leaf beater's skin. My cunt becomes a painstaking five-petalled flower made of hair—a Victorian mourning brooch, memento mori, enamelled gold frame rimmed in pearls. The dedication on verso reads *meminerunt omnia amantes*, lovers remember all.

Bedrest

makes me feel young again. 1980s young, specifically. Remember the fourth *Nightmare on Elm Street* when Joey dreams of a naked poster girl swimming inside his waterbed? Only seconds later, Freddy Krueger slaughters him in what might be the most perfect sexual arousal horror scene of all time. Rest has become Wes Craven–esque, all rubber reality and suffering stalking me in my sleep, all nocturnal emissions and neurotransmissions and tantrum.

In my somniloquence, I sing the lyrics to Van Halen's "Eruption." Neither starfish nor jellyfish are actually fish. Headcheese is meat. To pass time, I memorize all of Lurch's lines from *The Addams Family.* Neither peanuts nor coconuts are nuts. The French horn originated in Germany. So much stillness has taught my body how to cross over. The other side smells like diazepam drool on my pillowcase. It looks like dust particles slapdashing a sunbeam.

It's impossible to count the hairline cracks on my ceiling,

but I can imagine the horsehair woven into the old plaster. I can imagine the horses—haflingers with flaxen manes and tails—once very much alive and eager to enjoy an end-of-the-day ear of corn. The horizon line would have to be snow-blurred by cottonwood seeds. And running in dizzy circles in the pasture would feel delirious and safe.

Ibuprofen tablets contain corn syrup. Bleached wax too. Ibuprofen is coated in bleached wax. Pain management

is a teensy-weensy bit poisonous.

Horsehair plaster disappeared by the 1950s because better building materials were developed. Those materials were asbestos and lead.

Mortician's wax was famously used for torn flesh special effects in zombie films like the classic *Night of the Living Dead,* along with roasted ham and chocolate sauce. Wes Craven's signature blood was nothing but humble water and red food colouring. 500 gallons of red water were used in the original *Nightmare on Elm Street* alone. It sprays

his kill scenes like a burst water main,
like a loose firehose. Come on, sweet
flowing gore of my adolescence.

I google *thrombosis.* I google *weak bones*. I google *sedentary depression*. Moons
ago I wore a constant bruise below my clavicle bone

where my lover bit

down as I fucked her. The bruise radiated enough heat to coax me awake
in the middle of the night, which seemed so very romantic. In retrospect,
it might have been

a hematoma.

I'm told paranormal podcasts help release cortisol. This is a compelling theory,
but my fear response is defective so who cares. I am a ghost of my former self.
No matter how many meditation podcasts I listen to, my bed

never

becomes

a stratosphere of sublime noninquiry. The sweet illusory place where
there's nothing left to say "more" or "less" to, to say "zero" or "ten" to,
to say "flex" and "relax" to. So long, sonic demands. Farewell, wedge pillow.
Catch you on the rebound, haptic feedback.
Goodnight, light switch. Later, sippy cup.

My mattress cost more
than my wedding band.

In dreams

about driving, the gas pedal is pea soup.
Pea soup like Regan's famous vomit in *The Exorcist*.
Always this flowing gore, this stillness. In dreams,
my boot sloshes in the broth of it.

The Erotics of Chronic Pain #3

Pain initiates a threesome between my abstract and corporeal selves. Overdrawn lips, disordered amygdala, a bedridden pigeon—my thirst trap. Text back. I have fruit to jack. I lead a jackal pack. My desires have become progressively fantastic fauxtographs. Pork barrelling. Bacchanalia. How about you cast your lot with slap? I favour sex that is anaesthetic, or, at least, blackout orgasms are negotiable. My yum is counting backward from ten. I am granulation tissue dreaming of an infected wound. I am bedtime dreaming of beasthood. Of oxycodone dipped donkey dick. A triptych of choked rope. Tongue baths serviced by severed heads. An impossible leviathan stringing me up from teeth to asshole. My brain fucked out and saved in a jar of formaldehyde. Daddy, make me a wet specimen. Frankenstein's monster sprawled on an operating table is a hollow skull ready to be stuffed.

Really, I am alone
and scrolling impregnation
anime on my phone.

Unnamed Service Road

It's 2:56 and you are awake.
The pulse under your jaw throbs.
Carotid arteries throng your brain.
The senses reside here, below
your jaw, so does speech.
You say "service" aloud
like a wish.

The road, again. It empties
the air from your lungs. It smothers
you in and out of sleep. Deprivation
snare, a tight mesh.

It's 3:12 and you are awake.
You paddle your feet under the covers.
Your mouth tastes like gravel dust.

It's 3:27 and you are awake.
The things the road says to you
a thirsty loop, *I will widen you*
  like a horizon. I will mudhole you senseless.

It's 3:44 and you are awake.
Blue spots blotch the ceiling.
Your eyeballs itch. You reach for
the flashlight tucked under your pillow.

Pull. You leave the screen door
open behind you. It clacks against
the worn weatherstripping. Chickens
fuss the neighbours' coop. It's too hot
for the brood to roost. Dewless grass.
Dry earth crackles. Parched spring.
Summer already searing in.
The road says, *You better*
  pick up your pace.

It's 4:16 and you are awake.
Your flashlight catches
the eyeshine of some prairie animal—
badger or young coyote. The night
has stockpiled a startling bulk of stars.
Stones creep into your house slippers.

Endless mayflies coat the ground.
They refuse to flit out from under your feet,
their membranous wings stiff and reasonless.

The road welcomes you with a hiss.
Don't lose track of your surroundings,
you remind yourself. Are you dreaming? *No.*
What colour is the sky? *Bruise blue.*
Are there sounds? *Songbirds. Early*
-to-rise warblers. Are you alone? *Never.*

It's 4:24 and you brace for bitter force.
You are nervous because you know
that if you allow something big as a service
road to ruin you, you will end up crying.
You can't remember the last time you cried.
You've been holding for a long time.
You are holding now. Your knees
are tucked fetal under your chin.

The road holds too.
All night, it has held the heat
from yesterday's sun for you.
It is warm as it digs in. Be still.
If you buck in resistance your skin
will break against the gravel. Or buck,
scuff the unmarked parts of your body,
what does it matter now? Thrash
in this losing quarrel
with your unhallowed desires.

The road has taught the mayflies to sing,
their chorus: *I will take. I will take.*
The road has taught the spring heat wave
to douse you in spit. Humidity drip.
I've already used you up.

Something persistent yet unspeakable splits
the horizon. You say "yes,"
and still it's an intrusion.

It's 5:04 and you empty yourself
to accommodate the road. Inside out.
Double back. Lucidity collapse.
Sacral nerves lost in the washout dawn.
You are in another time frame.
A different geography.

Your first time with a girl
was on a gravel road just like this.
Just like this, but far enough away
that the daybreak birds were common crows,
not warblers, and the trees shed needles in the heat,
not leaves. As you pulled your teenage hand out
from under her denim skirt, she said,
"I swear I'll kill you if you tell anyone."
What devastation—a fifteen-year-old girl
threatening your life while her cum
is still webbed between your fingers.

It's 5:12 and you are awake.
Can you stand up again? Will you limp home
against the length of this unnamed service road?

Safe Space: A Monosyllabic Rewrite of Ann Cvetkovich's *An Archive of Feelings*

Indeed, the power of the notion of safe space resides in its double status as the name for both a space free of conflict *and* a space in which conflict and anger can emerge as necessary components of psychic resolution ... the pain and conflict inevitably unleashed when safe spaces are established, should be considered signs of success rather than failure.
—ANN CVETKOVICH, *An Archive of Feelings: Trauma, Sexuality, and Lesbian Public Cultures*

all we think of is safe space   we sing it in a round, *safe space*
queer space, our space, dear space   we slant the streets, we cry out "safe space
yes and yes, we want it and now!"   we chase time, we ask *when was safe space?*

each night we dream of safe space   it is far off and still strange to us
but at the edge of our dreams   stands the house of safe space
it is a two room house   both rooms are grand
the front room is for rest   the backroom is for fire

in the front room soft cots rim the walls   we can strip down in the front room
not a stitch, here our skins are lit   what bliss, this dream, we can love
and fuck in the front room   we can spread our legs
we can salt and pluck   we can tire ourselves out
it is safe to be tired here   in the front room we can sleep

in the backroom ash dots the air   flames lurch and hiss
we are prone to fear the backroom   but we need to burn
the felled trees of our past   we need the heat
to sweat out the old rot   from our own bones

in this dream, in the blaze   and awe filled backroom
we will hold smoke in our arms   we will give
each flame a name   we will make fire our kin

when we wake, and the sharp   world takes shape once more
we will ask ourselves, *what   did i dream of?*
and all at once, we will say "i dreamt of safe space
                                        you dreamt of safe space
                                                we dream of safe space."

Pink Disco

Lark, nice lark
Lark, I will pluck you
I will pluck your head
And your head. Lark!
—"ALOUETTE," Québécois folk song, translated from French

Think pink and misshapenly round
like butter mints stuck together
at the bottom of a crystal bowl
on some nonna's coffee table. Rockjaw
gnash, nonstop gnash. Aura migraine
and a diamond hard canine. Way back
they used to cut MDMA with ketamine.
But my drug nostalgia can get fucked.
Punked recall. I only went along on a
lark. Nice lark—

nice as a dose slipped in my drink.
The queer bar is funhousing again.
Bucking dance floor. Ball pit. Smells
like spandex lamé after the DJ mashes
Kylie Minogue's "Can't Get You Out
of My Head" with New Order's "Blue
Monday." I sound like someone who talks
about themselves in second person. Haze
summoner. You think it was such a great
lark? I will pluck you

from laxity, from bygones being bygones. Relive
gauche—that gay rumpus room with the knotty
pine panelling. Each knot a butthole
when the disco hits. Each knot god's mouth
with a blessed message. Yak in the sink,
my child. Cleanse. Absolve. A serotonin
baptism. God says, "I will be with you
as you walk through the fire." Then you say,
"I will pluck you from the fire, unscathed."
I will pluck your head

to safety before the skitches skitch.
Your brain's not yet sunny side in a skillet.
Dance into the sanctuary. Pockmarked
and fear not. A net is a ghost
but it will hold. Grind on boys in cut
off jean shorts. Pick their frayed edges
as they pluck your snarled yarn. Flip spit
in an unlit corner. Your lip gloss thinks
this is funny shit. Disco got your body
and your head. Lark!

Woe to the max.

At night, we'd go to the nearby high school and pretend
that I was Claire Standish and you were Brian Johnson

from *The Breakfast Club*. My taunts in your ear, remember?
You're totally barf. Do you have any idea how gross this is?

We knew John Hughes movies would not age well. Mean-
while I still have a fine pastel scar that cuts across my elbow.

I miss you. It sounds precious, or pining, but the feeling
is a KICK ME sign taped to my back, a recycled prank.

I was more prone to clanging at night. Haldol rhymes with scalpel,
rhymes with fragile, rhymes with battle, with fog bell and chock full.

Sometimes we would cry out, *the gods are watching*, as we
brought each other to climax. Except the only gods we knew

were First Evil and Glorificus from the Buffyverse. Death
is my gift. I'd wrap a fraught orgasm in kraft paper, if I could.

At night, we finger vaulted in the dyke bar's cloakroom. Sent spunk
smudged leather into the streets. We worked for seven dollars an hour.

I have nothing left to say to the mattress on the linoleum floor. But if
we were to reconcile, I'd recite all of Kathy Bates's lines from *Misery*.

At night, you fucked me like a heavy bag and before long a Bartholin's
cyst swelled up on the left side of my cunt. We both had unfortunate

flashbacks of watching *How to Get Ahead in Advertising* with our
drunken fathers as teens. Gen X is parasitic and don't get me started.

The truth is I still hear voices, only now they sound as far away
as Charlie Brown's parents. At night, we'd scale the white iron

fence to swim in the Super 8 pool. Your mermaid name was Baby
and my mermaid name was Johnny Castle. My mermaid name was Jack

and your mermaid name was Rose. Your mermaid name was Beavis
and my mermaid name was Butthead. We were role model poor

and nonsense rich. More than anyone else the ward psychiatrist
made me feel like I was in a Blockbuster movie. I preferred

your fist to tranquilizers. Less side effects. Until my midthirties
I lived as a heart-shaped Mylar balloon. I never thanked you

for tying the curling ribbon around your wrist. I'd like you to know
that I'm finally in my body now, and by "body" I mean the softest

bouncy castle you've ever celebrated a birthday in. Did you get
to turn thirty-five? Fifty? Are we both greying under the same moon?

Isn't it remarkable to be ɐlᴉʌə! I say to friends at lunch. We are
like a book club, except we soberly discuss near-death experiences.

You made me ejaculate while standing in front of our open window,
then used my hair to sop up the wet. After we were renovicted

and NIMBYS moved into our home, I'd like to think that traces
of my desiccated cum whispered insidious messages from under

the baseboards at night. *You will die. Your intestines will boil*
and writhe. Your brains will come out through your nose.

These memories are a havoc of ten-dollar prom dresses packed
on a thrift shop rack. I just googled *how can I repair loose sequins?*

I kept all your letters and lots of darkness too. You always
signed "the lunatic you're looking for" in place of your name.

Unfinished Poem

go-go boys coated in black light glitter ***shuttered*** the Hothead Paisan
lookalike dyke moshing to pop music ***shuttered*** the aging bait who wore
the same spandex shorts for a decade ***shuttered*** the inflatable sex doll
that always and inexplicably ended up on the dance floor ***shuttered***
ex sex in the cold storage ***shuttered*** Manic Panic tinged neck sweat
shuttered a queen named Shelly Frankenstein ***shuttered*** everyone
who knew the moves to Michael Jackson's "Thriller" on Halloween
shuttered snapping hand fans ***shuttered*** electric tape x nipple covers
shuttered The Castle ***shuttered*** Shaggy Horse ***shuttered*** the fae who made
you eat his candy necklace ***shuttered*** "Closer" by Nine Inch Nails ***shuttered***
"Spin Spin Sugar" by Sneaker Pimps ***shuttered*** looping *Liquid Sky* projected
on the wall ***shuttered*** looping *Paris Is Burning* ***shuttered*** Misty's Cabaret
shuttered Tino's Turkish Baths ***shuttered*** Pretty Faces ***shuttered*** Manhole
shuttered the disco ball ***shuttered*** rainbow ballon drop ***shuttered*** bubble machine
shuttered the green glass billiard lamp above the pool table ***shuttered*** the old
cis leather dyke and her transfemme wife who ran the place ***shuttered*** one burnt-
out tile on the illuminated dance floor ***shuttered*** Casablanca ***shuttered***
The Beaver ***shuttered*** The Bull Pen ***shuttered*** Candlelight Room ***shuttered***
Art & Pep's ***shuttered*** Madonna impersonators ***shuttered*** free condoms
shuttered STI testing site stickers on the washroom mirror ***shuttered*** "I am
lonely" written in black Sharpie on the stall wall ***shuttered*** LGBTQ2S+ crisis
line flyers spread around the tallboy tables ***shuttered*** *Hustler White* theme nights
shuttered the rough and dapper king who ran the place ***shuttered*** a windowless
basement with a smoke machine ***shuttered*** the bartender's silver skull ring
with a missing ruby glass eye ***shuttered*** the karaoke microphone's dented grill
shuttered naked vampires at the Hookers Ball ***shuttered*** a drink special called Ass
Juice ***shuttered*** all the Dollys on country night ***shuttered*** tipping Beyoncés
shuttered the bartender's leather Kangol hat ***shuttered*** the bartender's

tarot card tattoos, the Empress, the Hermit and the Tower ***shuttered***
"Gooba Gabba Gooba Gobble" scratched into the back door ***shuttered***
the rainbow choir singing "That's What Friends Are For" ***shuttered***
kissing booth fundraisers ***shuttered*** the anarcha-queer collective that ran
the place ***shuttered*** service bottom auctions ***shuttered*** cruising the smoke pit
in the alley ***shuttered*** the unsmoked cigarette tucked behind the bartender's
left ear ***shuttered*** gold link chains and diamond studs ***shuttered*** Drag Bingo
every Sunday ***shuttered*** Imperial Court pageantry ***shuttered*** busboys
in jockstraps ***shuttered*** pass the hat to fix the smashed window ***shuttered***
daddies who walked baby dykes to the bus stop at 3 a.m. ***shuttered*** the svelte
peddler who swept through at last call to sell dollar-a-stem roses ***shuttered***
everyone who knew the words to "Auld Lang Syne" on New Year's Eve
shuttered pink marabou feathers in beer puddles ***shuttered*** girls
who made you promise to text when you got home ***shuttered***
lost wigs ***shuttered*** phone numbers written in matchbooks
shuttered lipstick prints ***shuttered*** the slow dances
when we held each other after the music stopped

I wanted to write about the shuttering
of queer bodies or maybe something about how our doors
remain open as a collective metaphor, but really,
I have no idea how this poem ends.

When I wake up aching
and gulping air it is because
somnophilic witches
teamed me all night.

Selkie

Skins lay on the slippery rock like an empty dress. Sky clad,
famished. Skulk the shore without a stitch. Spring tide splits
your lip. Polaris force feeds you human language. The moon

invokes your turgid quim. Slip into mythos. Transform yourself
through unearthly means. Fury birth, bent wean, a nascent body
to hold old anger. Eddies swell into maelstroms when you sing.

Ships will perish. Men pulled into the depths. (Let's get this said
and done—the chronification of pain is an awful shapeshifter.
Thrust into an unknown form. Misdiagnosis, missed hemorrhage

in the imaging test, incongruous symptoms. Sick spin. Sick spin.
Begin again. Pain yarns a fantastic pornography if you listen.
To be monstrous is perverse medicine.) Seduce the first mortal

you see. Sturdy fishwife, thick and pretty slam piece. Strip her
to the scud with her own shucking knife. Raw trib her for hours
in the froth of an algae bloom. Her frail throat is your frail throat.

Her jawbone is your jawbone. Her sputtering cunt is your claim
to the human world. The slow syrup of her surrender makes you
hunger for the next. You want to devour every warm gorgeous thing

in your path. Sea slew, rocks off. You want to doom harbours, flood
coastal towns. You want to rule the damage. Queen over a suffering
that is not your own. You want ruin. You want to return to the water.

Swan Maiden

/aw /ow /au /oo / her gliding vowels, a curious trumpet
i will eat her sounds like skiff beetles below the surface
she can't hold her breath underwater for long

my feather vestment shed, and she, bare as a skipping
stone, woven clothes thrown to the shoreline columbine
/aw /ow /au /oo / her gliding vowels, a curious trumpet

dulcet frailbait, a mortal snike with cygnus lust, we sink
into the still basin. down down, heavy brine at the bottom
she can't hold her breath underwater. for long

or not for long in this form, i best stir both hands while i
have them, quick churn. her spellbound pulp to gobble
/aw /ow /au /oo / her gliding vowels, a curious trumpet

curious limbs and skin, curious purse as easy as flying
through shapeless april air. so keen for my preening, but
she can't hold her breath underwater for long

waterlogged, but lanced on my wingspan. a lake is a thrash
house, sweet choke home. i carry her over the threshold
/aw /ow /au /oo / her gliding vowels, a curious trumpet
she can't hold her breath underwater for long

Lewis Carroll Could Never

bandersnatch   snark   carving fork   frolic

she has the tits of a dream girl and four sick
stomachs stuffed with cud   tunnel gut allegory
her cool moobox destroyed by subhuman truth

nonsense nightmare or nut nap   it's all gothic
buttermilk to me   all schmoopy soup and girl
friend noodles   she has the syrinx of a canary
and sings rainbows in the basin   half dipper
doe her name femanon thingamabob   doojigger

whatsherface a slithy mystery   her front is one
animal her rear is another   grotesque conquest
the glad rapture of the hunt   she has restless
giddy-up legs and the keloid scars of a   dumb

slut   if snark be a snark then mutt be a mutt
snallygaster be snallygaster   catawampus
be catawampus   romancing the portmanteau

c'mere chimera moonbait bouf   untouched woo
woo swoop   oofable as an angora rabbit
and she bites if startled   she has a mind like fallow
wheat and might like a good thundering

this tricky grift   oh, to one day catch
her fine angelwine
and even finer bafflement

Janara

Unguento, unguento,	Ointment, trip ointment,
portami al noce di Benevento,	carry me to the walnut tree of Benevento,
sotto l'acqua e sotto il vento,	under the water and under the wind,
sotto ogni maltempo	under all bad weather.

—LITURGICAL SONG, circa seventh century, from somewhere
in the Lombard Kingdom, Italy

Broomstick. Golden snake slipped my dewy v
—is for viper. Worship. I woke up in the crotch
of a walnut tree. Temporal blur, last night, all
my sisters turned themselves into snakes.
Cast skins, an ecdysis pleasure. To be born
again, but will this time really be different?
Disfigure me, please. Mix a rich trip:
belladonna, henbane, jimson, mandrake,
parsnip, poppy, thorn apple, wild mint.
Ointment, trip ointment,

ritual smear, under arms and over my other
hairy places. Tingling dose. Divine
fraggle, dazzle the watching gods.
Now my cunt speaks garglefunk. A call-
and-response song—gargle in the bell
tower, gargle down the shallow creek,
gargle in the goat shack, gargle through
my open window. They enter as wind.
Spangled mist sisters, lucent as a lunar halo,
carry me to the walnut tree of Benevento.

Hang my clothes from its green branches.
Broadleaf canopy and fissured bark, blessed.
Back at the Sabbath again, out where a fiend
is a fiend. Swill wisdom, glug, glug.
Spitfix my soused mouth. Triple
grease me in witch butter. Plump my skin
like a spring sow. Indoctrination by excess,
by synapse overflow. Pychotrop my fertile v
—is for vision. Now my cunt slowgrinds
under the water and under the wind,

under the fire and under earth. Sub
rosa sprawl, a plundering panorama.
Do diabolical things, my sisters. Turn me
edgeways, supine in the stomping circle.
Team me as rooster and rabbit, as rabid
hags, spectral slog knobs, breathing fever.
Tomorrow, I may wake in the Sabato River,
but tonight smother me under the hours,
under sadness and flux, under pleasure and
under all bad weather.

Canidia

One of the witches cried out to Hecate. The other to cruel Tisiphone. You might have seen snakes and hell-hounds wandering around, a blushing Moon, hiding behind the tall tombs, so as not to be witness.
—HORACE, *The Satires,* translated by A.S. Kline

Gash flash, barefoot in the borderlands,
a bone path beaten by thieves and beasts
and me, drenched in rancid midnight.

Predatory magic. Scruff of a wolf's neck,
guard hairs in my greedy hands. Snakes
drained of venom. Blood lamb brew.

Love potion and poison are the same cup.
Minds turned by sweet talk or tricky incantation.
A wax effigy and a husband both catch fire.

The republic others me—hag on their lips, they
speak in smear and order. Still, I unright the divide.
Nocturnal service mixed in a scrubbed necropolis.

I pull down the moon, goon her dark side,
her borrowed light is a ghost ride. Gibbous
thrust, bump her compass unconscious.

East and West swap sides. Watchmen are lost
beneath these upset stars. Silver kissed
horizon. It's safe to come out now, sisters.

Come to the gardens of Maecenas. Come
barefoot and filthy. Spit on arched limestone
as you pass through the Esquiline gate.

This lavish estate was raised on our lovers' graves.
Convicts and slaves, peasant soldiers and seers—
all thrown in the republic's scavenger pit.

Come bald the greenbelt. Bare-knuckle dig.
Root out tamed periwinkle and knapweed.
Pour gore and wine and honey on the upset soil.

Sing to the stirring dead. Unsettled requiem.
Crude cymbals and bells. Scent the night
with fescennine and love song. Cold kiss.

Strip off mortal rags. Serve your raw bodies
for the funerary feast. A ceremony to slab
stunt and tender. Our union is a cipher.

It is a wisdom hidden by the weight of day.
I stretch the dark hours, porous and vile. Thin.
I will hold the shadows until my fingers shiver.

Rot rub in the underworld. Grind our shared
grief until it pulps. Pleasure seethe one last time.
Through us, our lovers' ghosts will cross over.

Henry Fuseli

Titania and Bottom, 1790

If we shadows have offended,
Think but this, and all is mended,
That you have but slumbered here
While these visions did appear.
—WILLIAM SHAKESPEARE, *A Midsummer Night's Dream*

Faerie characters really wronghorn me, crotch ticklers,
but here goes. Let's dose ourselves with wild pansy, pink
-of-my-john drops, the same spell that Puck spat
in Titania's eye. Love spell, sometimes a painkiller.
Misplaced magic. How many fae fit on the head of a pin?

Our donkey-faced groom and the winx who loves him.
Braying plainsong, from forelock to muzzle, pure sorcery.
Bottom's shag coupled with Titania's irrational beauty.

Midsummer Night coupled with May Day, narcotic time
rift, woodland rite on a loop. Light coupled with cast
shadow, reverse halo, Fuseli's chiaroscuro of unconscious.

How many blackout days will bring another moon?

Why don't we wedge in with this grotesque company?

The waxen changeling scowling in our direction can't be all bad. The miniature hermit on a leash, Mustardseed and Moth, Peaseblossom and Web, they seem friendly.

If not friendly, at least fun. What kind of fun? Depraved, I hope. Why else would so many slinky faebies show up clothed in white organza—breezy nipple display, troupe of fragrant nosegays, of brat handlers. This scene is love.

This dream is freakish love, that's why we recognize it. Lavish vicious love, cuck and bull love, sideways hearth love, blood and spoonful love. We've tasted sour love before. We've gagged on the same backward prayer. Our doll and maker love, whirligig and habituation love, our pith and nub love. We're one with this seditious love.

If I desire
women who are fiction,
does it mean
I have fictionalized myself?

Hostile Architecture

I've learned to live with the inevitability of a third armrest.
Actually, that's a tired lie. I haven't learned to live.

I haven't learned to distinguish myself
from the surroundings. I am something
like stripped timber screws and pressure
treated skin, a thermoplastic-coated steel
pubic crest. Centre bar split, a magician's
assistant perpetually being sawed in half
abracadabra
hostile architecture

I haven't learned to live
in the city that caps the shaded
anchor of Ironworkers Bridge in concrete teeth.
Store frontages along Main edged with stone spikes

abusing the system is an oxymoron
Is *breaking the law*?
Is it reasonable to overidentify with park benches?
Are move-along orders reasonable or un?
The police force calls displacement soft tactics,
the city calls it design.

Once I stood in a gutted bus shelter with an old-timer
drinking soup kitchen coffee in Styrofoam cups. We recited
the Serenity Prayer, our common balm, our last gasp solace
the serenity
the things I cannot change

Once I was loitering.
Actually, that's a tired lie or a federal law, same difference.
Once I was charged with loitering. Stop-
and-frisk street check on the corner of Semlin and Pandora.
a disturbance or obstruction
no peace, no quiet. I was
something like suspicious circumstances and reasonable
grounds, a mental danger. I was a teenage girl.

A body is a running expense.
Is *spare change* an oxymoron?
Who's got change just lying around?
Who's got change?

In this city, public space is malignant. Abnormal mass
spreading to bone and nerve and it hurts to lie

down.

A third armrest
is never about rest.

YOUR PARTICIPATION IS VOLUNTARY

My medical study consent form amended as a Star Trek *data module file.*

You are being contacted by the research team at the Xenobiology Unit of the United Federation of Planets because you are eligible to participate in the Protomorphosis Syndrome Study (protomorphotropic determinants of genetic alteration) research study.

You have the right to refuse to participate in the study. If you decide to participate, you may still choose to withdraw at any time without any negative consequences to your biobed or other treatments to which you are entitled or which you are presently receiving. Your treatment will be the same, regardless of whether you join (or do not join) the Protomorphosis Syndrome Study. We plan to continue collecting data as long as this Xenobiology Unit is in existence.

Before you decide, it is important for you to understand what the study involves. This consent form will tell you about diagnostic test studies, including tissue scans, medical tricorder analysis, and subdermal bioprobes, why these tests are being done, what will happen to you during the tests, and the possible benefits, risks, and discomforts.

If you wish to participate in this Protomorphosis Syndrome Study, you can consent through a Code 3 link found in the holo-communicator.

Please take time to read the following information carefully and to discuss it with your family, friends, and commanding officer before you decide.

WHO IS CONDUCTING THE TISSUE SCAN?

On Stardate 4679.1, the Federation provided funding for formal development of a dedicated interdisciplinary Protomorphosis Syndrome Program. The study is being conducted by Dr. Beverly Crusher, Dr. Phlox, and Dr. T'Ana, as well as Counsellor Troi, an Emergency Medical Hologram, and other sickbay personnel. All sickbay personnel in this field are extremely knowledgeable in the xenobiology of a numerous species—both humanoid and not—as well as viruses and diseases native to dozens of worlds.

Scans are conducted at Starbase 84 Surgical Sickbay, Xenobiology Unit, United Federation of Planets.

BACKGROUND

Protomorphosis Syndrome (at least 6 months duration) affects 25% of non-human species of Starfleet and close to 15% of all non-humans and can have a devastating impact on quality of life.

Early symptoms include abnormal behaviour, irritability, hyperactivity or decreased activity, pelvic pain, chills, loss of mobility, difficulty sitting, urinary incontinence, constipation and dyschezia, loss of pleasure during sex, loss of short-term memory, genetic reversal, personality changes, hair loss, diminished fingernail growth, cell mutation, morphing into spider, jellyfish, or apelike creatures, bleeding, prolapse, exoskeleton shattering, and fever.

WHO CAN PARTICIPATE IN THIS STUDY?

Any non-human Starfleet personnel referred to the Xenobiology Unit, regardless of showing symptoms of Protomorphosis Syndrome or not.

WHAT DO THE TESTS INVOLVE?

If you agree to participate in the study, we will store your holo-questionnaire responses and clinical data from your tissue scan, tricorder analysis, bioprobe, and other test results on Memory Alpha. If applicable, further tests include but are not limited to: physical examination, biochemistry sample collection, tissue collection, electromyonic sensor analysis, gene analysis, and the use of cortical stimulators, delta-wave inducers, dermal regenerators, and exoscalpels.

You will receive additional follow-up holo-questionnaires approximately 6 months, 1 year, 2 years, 3 years, 4 years, and 5 years after the first scan.

WHAT HAPPENS IF I DECIDE TO WITHDRAW MY CONSENT TO PARTICIPATE?

You may withdraw from the study at any time without giving reasons. If you agree to the study and then decide to withdraw at a later time, you have the right to request the withdrawal of your collected data.

Please note, however, that there may be exceptions where the data will not be able to be withdrawn. For example, where the data is no longer identifiable, meaning your samples have undergone genetic mutation, or where the data has merged with other participants' samples.

If you would like to request the withdrawal of your data, please let a chief medical officer or the Emergency Medical Hologram know.

CAN I BE ASKED TO LEAVE THE SICKBAY?

There are no circumstances where you might be asked to leave.

WHAT HAPPENS IF SOMETHING GOES WRONG?

We do not anticipate any harms or discomforts from participating in the scan. However, amniotic fluid retrovirus injections, plasma infusion, delta-wave induction, tissue mitigation, dermal regeneration, or other surgical interventions may be required.

Signing this consent form in no way limits your sentient rights as protected by the Charter of the United Federation of Planets.

AFTER THE TISSUE SCAN IS FINISHED

In the future, we may conduct further scans to better understand Protomorphosis Syndrome and other xenobiological viral syndromes that are unrelated to this study (e.g., randomized controlled trials). Please indicate below if we may contact you regarding future scan studies:

☐ Yes, contact me regarding future scan studies.
☐ No, do NOT contact me regarding future scan studies.

CONSENT TO PARTICIPATE

My signature on this consent form means:

- I have read and understood the information and the consent form.
- I have had the opportunity to ask questions and have received satisfactory responses from sickbay personnel.
- I understand that data collected will be kept confidential within Memory Alpha.
- I understand that my participation is voluntary and that I am completely free to withdraw at any time.
- I understand that there is no guarantee that this study will provide any benefits to me.

____

Participant's signature   Printed name   Date

IT

Pain is not a clown.
Pain is an ancient evil as old as the universe itself.
Pain emerged from a void larger than the entirety of existence.
Pain named this cosmic infinite-beyond-infinite void the Body.
Pain itself is also the Body. Body is a living pocket dimension of Body.
Pain, in turn, is a living pocket dimension of Pain.
Pain fled the void at an unknown point in time and travelled across space.
Pain was brought to Earth by an incomprehensible cataclysmic event.
Pain slumbered beneath the Earth's crust for millions of years.
Pain awoke at the arrival of humankind, hungry and malevolent.
Pain malforms itself into our worst fears.
Pain shows us a maddening glimpse of the void that is Pain.
Pain does not need food to survive. It preys on us for its own pleasure.
Pain, in fact, does not eat us alive. It consumes our fear and the process is fatal.
Pain primarily appears in the form of Pennywise the Dancing Clown, but
Pain is not a clown.
Pain is an ancient evil as old as the universe itself.
Pain emerged from a void larger than the entirety of existence.
Pain named this cosmic infinite-beyond-infinite void the Body.
Pain, itself, is also the Body.

PINHEAD

Hemorrhage's ontology is difficult to explain. **Hemorrhage**

has been called a rhapsodic and grotesque
exploration of sadomasochism. Some believe

Hemorrhage was once flesh and blood, a soul who lost
faith in god. This origin story positions **Hemorrhage**

as an incarnation of flesh and blood. After shattering
the schism between human and posthuman existence,

Hemorrhage was unbound by the laws of the universe.
This assumed lawlessness, however, disregards **Hemorrhage**'s

religious proclivities and the observance of rituals
and practices, beliefs and teachings, sacred places
and sacred objects therein. Demonologically speaking,

Hemorrhage is a Cenobite. **Hemorrhage**

resides in a monastic shadow realm
ruled by the hell god, Leviathan.

Hemorrhage is Pontifex of the Order of the Gash. **Hemorrhage**

has taken a vow of ritual torture.
Qualitative evidence suggests that

Hemorrhage targets those whose transgressions
involve the pursuit of pleasure. **Hemorrhage**'s

prevailing method of attack is to trap his victims
in an eternity of pain rather than to outright kill. But what

Hemorrhage inflicts is a physical experience
beyond pain, beyond the sensory. **Hemorrhage**'s

sadomasochism is ecstatic, in that pain
and pleasure are indivisible. It follows that

Hemorrhage aims to liberate his victims. **Hemorrhage**

is famously quoted as saying,
"Your flesh is killing your spirit."

SKEKSIS

towering
reptilian
vulturine
Neuroendocrine Tumors
send a zombie army
marching into the spitter pit
mind controllers, phony
caretakers of the once-
healing Crystal
feigning benevolence
order
divine right
immortals
on a wasted planet
gangrenous flesh and atrophied
limbs garbed in red velvet
barbaric absolutes, supremacists
at a banquet table feasting
on the last lifeblood, the last
piths of the nearly extinct
vestigial limbs, numb claws
still grabbing at shortages
Neuroendocrine Tumors
came to betray, without
reason, without need
annihilation
in a glass vessel
the last slave drained
of her essence

The Dark Crystal is the only movie from my childhood that I refuse to watch again. I was nine years old when it came out on VHS. I don't remember being afraid then (not like when my ma let me watch *Poltergeist* that same year, and I began pinching myself, hard, in bed to blunt the night terrors). As an adult, though, the dreadful Skeksis tramp through my anxious thoughts. I didn't have a kittens and skipping rope childhood, but I wasn't prepared to see nearly all life destroyed on the planet Thra.

The stakes are unthinkably high, not only for a kids' film, but for any film. Jim Henson wanted to scare children; he didn't think it was healthy for children to always feel safe. I'm inclined to agree, although I can't actually conceive of what it means to "always feel safe," so my agreement is open to question. I suppose we all have that one film from childhood that destroyed us. I supposed that film destroyed us because it showed us the gruesome things we'd soon learn about the world. Does being an unsafe child better prepare you for the unsafe world? Hmm, I guess I don't really know what I agree with.

Which childhood film destroyed you?

To this day, imagining the Skeksis' brutal decaying bodies still triggers a disorienting grief response. I doubt the Skeksis can be made into metaphor. I probably shouldn't include this poem in my collection.

XENOMORPH

(from the Greek *xeno-*, meaning "other" or "strange,"
and *-morph*, meaning "transformation")

Ovomorph

            the genesis
    of sickness.
                    Leathery
membrane and albumen
a sentient egg.   Living
pathogen and chokepoint.
A trap laid one thousand years ago
sickness recognizes your vibration
scent and body heat.
                            Blood
hatchling. Acid afterbirth.

Sickness latches on
to the nearest host.
Second stage in a life cycle
of hostility, of predation.

Facehugger.

Tail around your neck.
Maw assault.
A mesoskeletal breathing tube
crams your throat. Put to strangled
sleep with alien chloroform.
Sickness only lets go
after implanting
the embryo.

Sick infant.

            Chestburster

chews through
                        rib cage
             spinal cord
  pelvic girdle.
Your ilium and cartilage—
sicknesses' first sustenance.
Fresh born
pale and limbless.

Indescribable taxonomy
   a brutal liver fluke
   opium asp
   bone eel dashing the corners

 Sickness will hide
 until fully grown.

Mature sicknesses
are solitary

warriors.

Stealthy, hard targets
but will attack en masse
to protect the hive.
Piston-tongued and projectile
inner jaw. Eyes hidden behind
their vacuum black carapace.
Sickness can eradicate whole
civilizations
in a single day.

Sickness
will capture instead of kill
when the hive requires
a fresh cache
of living hosts.

Queen

            sickness lays
eggs by the hundreds. Life cycle
restock, like the generation
before and the generation
before immemorial, this sickness
will assume the biological
traits of the hosts
who spawn them.
Which means
more and more
sickness looks
like you.

Pain is really into dollification
but I'm tired of being costumed in human skin.
Ersatz and pretty-witted boredom. I need to be beaten
back into my true form.

depersonalization is an altered state of identity #2

I am soft and lacy and space is far more arduous than I expected.
Infiniteness is no tickle. No joke. No one promised me a tomorrow.

I am free. And by free, I mean far from people. And by people, I mean
dumb lumbering bodies who don't know what to do with their hands.

I am hallowed and holy and have been snatched by the cosmos.
I should turn myself inside out before my velvet nap wears thin.

Fact: There are more trees on earth than stars in the milky way.
I am alone and searching for a lover made of stardust: Fiction.

Space is completely silent and a pipe organ is a big box of whistles. /ə/
is the most common vowel in the English language and I miss the voice of god.

Medications that cause hair loss:

infliximab

warfarin

heparin

methotrexate

perindopril

lisinopril

A jackdaw plucks me in rough tufts
from an Appaloosa's withers.
Soon I'll be the lining of a fool's nest.
Burdened by specked eggs
come spring, then hungry noise.
Curse her naked hatchlings' chatter.
Swans will speak when jackdaws are silent.

etanercept

sulfasalazine

leflunomide

valproic acid

carbamazepine

divalproex sodium

cimetidine

ibuprofen

naproxen

aspirin

Why is hair pulling so rashly gratifying?
Inanimates reach consciousness
just for the pleasure of pulling me out.
I'm caught in her leather buttoning.
Studs and piping have their kinks too.
I no longer belong to myself. I am
the filthy keepsakes of a chesterfield sofa.

haloperidol

chlorpromazine

olanzapine

quetiapine

risperidone

lamotrigine

propranolol

metoprolol

amitriptyline

venlafaxine

escitalopram

Those who shed hair and skin
are immortal. Shapeshifting Good Walkers
saw five centuries of lauding whispers,
but what about the wolf pelts
left in the shade of a spruce grove?
Who remembers us?
I was a witch's armour once.

Ember Sabbath. I bristled
as she crowned the clouds.
Ours was a battle for the moon itself.
The valour of it all, only to be left
alone and uninhabited by daybreak.
She did not bother to bury me,
my witch. I turned into fine wisps,
then a meagre feast for the beetles.

lithium

vinorelbine

doxorubicin

nilotinib

paroxetine

levodopa

mirtazapine

vortioxetine

ozempic

leflunomide

I am blond and boxed in museum glass.
White-gloved handlers tour me across
the salesroom floor. Dogging
Sotheby's auction house, I coax
philharmonic nostalgia. Melodic lust
steams my display case. I would give
myself to paddle number 141. She covets

my flute magic. I feel her soprano wagging
for my twisted tongue and sing, patter
patter, patter, sing, patter. *Un desio*
che lei non possa spiegar. A desire
she cannot explain costs a small fortune.

oestrogen

progestin

anabolic steroids

Chilly Down

I'm not special. Everyone who took the "Which *Labyrinth*
Character Are You?" quiz wanted to be the Fireys. Hedonists
in red pelts. Hyperbolic beasts, I wish. And have wished
and will wish, infinity. Zoh my, those fire muffs.
Fawking gawd, scuzzy shags of the forest.

What is your fashion style? a) plastic jewels b) seven-sock
packer c) billowing white taffeta d) ain't got clothes
to worry about. Who wouldn't streak with the fire gang?
I'm already nake and brainless. Already thrown in the head.
I already do think bent with the fire gang.

Which way do you want to go? a) up b) down c) HELP
d) You're hurting me! Unfasten my morphology. I want
to unrig myself without ache or damage. Picture my limbs
juggled like bowling pins. Eyeballs rimming
a roulette wheel. A bobblehead to pass and be caught.

Alley-oop. Fun and games. Only fun and games.
There are no bad bets in the fire gang. No bad choices.
No consequence. Nobody cutting a deal with pain meds.
Nobody negotiating a short-term treatment plan.
No bad days. There are no bad bodies
in the fire gang. No bad heads in the fire.

An apple a day keeps the doctor away.
I mean, a sqountch a day keeps the doctor away.
How about we pervert every trite line about health?
You are what you skeet. Fit as a fiddler. Let's rough
up platitudes. *Time paraphils all wounds.*
What doesn't kill you makes you monster.
I want to be shown a good time.

Your ideal lover is ...? a) anyone
who will love you, fear you, do as you say
b) the dazed starlet at a masquerade ball c) an anonymous
stranger in an oubliette d) a swapmeat of detached limbs.

If you think you're the only bedrest sogging off
to appendage orgies, I promise you're not.
Maybe everyone who's woken up on an operating table
fantasizes about reattaching limbs wherever we please.
When you're alone, remember the magnificent oaf pack
around you. When you think you're ruined,
be even more ruinous. Think devastation, be free.

Someone is trying to take off your head,
what do you do? a) run in the opposite direction
b) I've been through worse c) LET THEM
d) Who really gets to keep their head these days anyway?

It's an old dilemma—do I want to be *with* a Firey
or do I want to *be* a Firey? Would I rather
be a headless body or a bodyless head? Be roasted
or be the flames? Picture my fingers as torches
slowly smouldering down to the stave. Hips
so loose that my legs fall away. I want to lull
and chill with the fire gang. Hair down
with the fire gang. Tits out, chin up. Tongue
slipped with the fire gang. Brain picked
with the fire. Sent up with the fire.

The *Twin Peaks* Theme Song

Friends warned that I wouldn't be well enough to write and I took their word. Real spit, I've never been a henchman to a first draft. I easily untangle my worth from creative output. So, I had no productive recovery delusions of mapping my novel, absolutely no goals to make bedrest my bitch. My post-op plan was to binge the Emmy-winning shows that everyone talks about—*Fargo* or *The Marvelous Mrs. Maisel* or whatever, *The Bear.* I didn't make it through a single pilot episode. Dialogue clumped together like wet sand. A plots spun out immediately. B plots, nonexistent. I couldn't handle new characters. Couldn't even learn their names. My intestines were literally shifting position. Maybe peritoneum membranes were regrowing? I'm not sure what went down with the visceral gunk inside me. To console myself, I read a study—by which I mean I skimmed the abstract—that claimed immersion into familiar fictional worlds restores self-control.

Turns out, I needed familiar
weird and familiar pain
while gliding hydromorphone.

Dale Cooper's familiar voice immediately inundated my numb. Donuts wreathed my throb. In the fictional town of Twin Peaks, the waterfall still falls. Sycamore trees still grow in rings. A forever-grey sky looms. The owls still aren't what they seem. The comfort of a cruel undertow. Eerie vertigo, a deluge of rich rich nowhereness. Agents still search Lynch's anxious frontier, high and low. Femme and forest-still dark forces. Stolen shadows, stolen pages from Laura Palmer's secret diary, stolen, stolen. And Laura Palmer! And Laura Palmer, still my dream girl. We were the same age when I first watched the show. Sweet sixteen. Twinned and tortured, my love. Familiar as a hopeless crush. Laura Palmer still says, "When you see me again, it won't be me." Except in reverse. Everyone in the Black Lodge still swivels backward speech.

EEm eb t-now ti, geyn-ah EEm ees OOy nEW.
I rediscovered phonemes like discovering
prophecy in a blue rosebud.

I know my way to the teeth of the spectral cave. Threshold callback. Gladly, I turn in a maze of twitchy red curtains. Malevolent jazz dances me across the zagging floor. Deviant muscle memory. A routine pass around the Black Lodge. Doppelgäng me, please. Pain has already made me a double. One self enjoys a damn fine cup of coffee, while the other warps sound in an extra-dimension. One self skinny-dips in a shallow stream, the other gags on the name of my killer. Chronic pain is a fire walk between worlds. All pain is a fire walk. I'll only bring this up once, I first saw *Twin Peaks* in a house where my teenage body was BOBed, vesselled, possessed, you get it, enough said. Maybe rewatching it with a lacerated vaginal canal—and other sufferings—wasn't my best move? What have I learned about boundaries? What do we actually know about duality, about ununited cosmology? Laura Palmer and I have been parasocially dating since high school and she still won't marry me. Surrogate truelove. Familiar enigma. Is it fair to categorize *Twin Peaks* as trauma erotics? Am I always going to return to trauma erotics?

I still want the man from another place
to spit garmonbozia in my mouth.
But more gently this time.

Listen, I'm not really into othering myself. I already wrote a memoir and toured around to tell audiences about the fantastic faith I have in my enduring cunt. I am not special and *Twin Peaks* is no silo. No surreptitious niche. It was prime time. Franchised. Merchandized. You can buy a Funko Pop collectible figurine of Laura Palmer's dead body, for fuck's sake. You can't spin a ceiling fan without hitting a survivor with an affinity for *Twin Peaks*. I'm stomping the stomping ground. I'm copying a reproduction. Repeating gabble. She's filled with secrets: *Sir-kith thew lift-see essh.* Pastiche-meld me again. And, yeah, maybe trauma erotics were more poignant when the pilot aired in 1990? During the height of laissez-faire capitalism, who didn't need to see a severed stag's head unceremoniously plonked in a bank? The treasured oracle crone cradling a log entered our homes alongside Prozac and the 24-hour news cycle. We ate Lynchian surrealism like cherry pie. Rooms within rooms within realms. Psycho pop. Soapy amoral balm. Camp-o-drama. And a killer so beyond description that we gladly latched on to non sequiturs instead. What I rewatched during my recovery was generational silence. Close-up after close-up of hyped crying made me remember how willing we were to spoof grief. Familiar as a hopeless crush. The pain of living tissue.

The *Twin Peaks* theme song triggers
a Pavlovian response. Feels like stolen ground.
Nothing to really hold me. Are we falling in love?

Cosmological Touch

To mitigate this pain you must massage the void.
Never mind glossing the abdomen in almond oil, hot
compress, menthol temples, fine milled licorice root,
never mind fascia and muscle. It's all carnal noise.

It's all racket and backache, spasm and babble.
To mitigate this pain you must massage the void.
Anything of clay or split fruit, egg or hominid—
let go. You're already reaching for the unreachable.

These are not directives of nihilism and despair.
In negative decibels, in intangible density, rejoice.
To mitigate this pain you must massage the void.
Emptiness is an erogenous zone, a collapsed star,

black with absence and oxytocin. Sanctify and toy,
lubricate the dark energy. A body transposed by pitch
and edge. Love transforms you into what you love.
To mitigate this pain you must massage the void.

Our swollen tongues brunch in the underworld.

No, I won't tell you how Persephone takes her eggs.
Everyone is so nosy these days. Leave us to feast
in peace. Leave us to our own private realm of yolk

and white, of spoil and the unripe, of force
and weightlessness, of fluency and the inaudible.
I could go on, but these are easy paradoxes. Dull Sunday
kind of paradoxes. The current moment is an unlit labyrinth
at last call on a Friday night and each one of us has lost
cell service and our keys and faith in a certain tomorrow.

What a tangle. The current moment is a mud nest clinging
to concrete. Confused cliff swallows, all of us, we built
our nests upside the trophy penthouse on Park Avenue.
The thing is we never did manage to eat the rich.

We should be cribbing active volcanoes.
We should be liberating the abyss.
We should be undergrounding the underground. Deep. Deep.
The excavation of our desire is a risky dig. Groundwater
and angry fossils slow us down. But Deep. And Deep. Please.

The Mariana Trench looks like a good brunch spot.
We can make it work. We've frequented worse.
Away from unwanted eyes. Away from oxygen.
Leave us to the density of the ocean. Leave us
to generate our own light. Bioluminescence
around a table. Banquet of Hades. Every myth
about the underworld belongs to us now.
The River Styx and the Isles of the Blessed—
leave those narratives with us. Deep. Deep.
Leave us to our own electricity.

Stable in the Sky

the orion nebula once had a beloved leather bar
the spanking bench alone was legendary
        stalwart slab
        good heavens
        we were immobilized comets
        vapour tails in ankle cuffs
    we saw poseidon's trident dipped in crisco
the depth of desire can be elbow or abyssal

  but not infinite
  the bar closed in the early 2000s

                                    it all comes down
to a cosmic tug-of-war
to keep the doors open
                                    fucking

rent rent fucking rentfucking rent
                                    is anyone currently
in space right now?   does anyone
remember subspace?

                                    was it a null
in the matrix kind of subspace or was it an all-out
adrenal-dump kind of subspace?

was it edge play or was it cusp season?
were we bound by vacuum beds or in vacuums devoid of matter?

anyway

remember

hellenistic wisdom can really eclipse
your mind during a machofemme takedown

naked eye   naked eye   naked eye astronomers
are greedy bottoms
skylicking asteroid dust
bootblacking dark matter

the ceremony   the pageantry   the worship
what a sight!

but still

there is this ongoing personal dilemma of loneliness

the stars these days are only like 15 billion years old
has the past lost its power? has our hydrogen burnt out?
where is the rotational speed that once kept us together?
are we becoming an unseen mass?

but still

a solar flare or an expanding sun or the last
stages of an impending stellar giant could wipe us out
we never saw it coming is subterfuge

leather queers
don't look at the night sky and wonder what will kill us
we're already collared to catastrophe

besides

catastrophe is an overturning, a reverse course
from the greek *katá* (over) *stréphō* (I turn)
switchy ritual

besides

how lucky you are   lucky lucky you
your fixed stars were once stroked
fingers have banged all four quadrants in three houses
you've stuffed your supermoon with gut feelings

and you still walk backward into any bedroom
counter magic practice
backmask danger words until all is   hum

empty what's stuck
reverse penetration with

deep

slow

breaths

yes

this is a roman trumpet

a signal

a sign

a three-pitched whistle

a call to remember
that two humble donkeys helped defeat the titans
don't give up on the celestial manger

plug your mouth with spring clover
plunge your hands into interstellar water
handball your own gravity

remember
we're still a cancer of crabs pinching each other
you're still a circular clearing in the forest
a stroll
a stomp
a method of divination
get into it

start squaring
triangulating
quadrupling pop
multi-dimensional portal season always comes back

seek pleasure in saturn   or wherever whenever
be DTFreeFall

the backrooms are in retrograde   the next equinox
will be a total perve   bratty borealis will glorify
the sky   see it?
see it?
seers soothsay what?

just stay curious

look up

look up

starry starry cluster
sploshing constellations
nova   pop   pop

full orbit
at the end of winter crone passes maiden a red silk ribbon

at the mouth of the river a nymph and grindylow
wait for you to third their sludgeboxes

at the rim of every spigot you are welcome
to chug fountain water
stay thirsty or feast   be fluid or starve

but put the halter back on the beast
ride until you careen into darkness

remember
the gods turned two humble donkeys into stars
to thank them for braying loud enough to win a war

Asellus Borealis and Asellus Australis

the whole universe loves a noisy whore
the whole universe loves you

depersonalization is an altered state of identity #3

I wait at the centre of the universe, which is also an altar of sorts. Chain
hill click clicks a hymn. My shadow looks like a row of steepled teeth.

My desire is so dark, it's gravitational. Bent light. Time pulled
into taffy. We only need heat and sugar to understand abundance.

Mercury may be the god of speed, but I can make brains bleed in less
than eighty seconds. I identify as plummet mother, a she-bop-a-woo-bop.

Yes, I put out on the first drop. I identify as a misnomer. The universe
does not have a centre. No edge either. The universe is not expanding

from anywhere and it's not expanding into anything. Facts. Screams
are studied in small padded rooms. Screams are measured in decibels.

I identify as louder than a chainsaw and softer than a comet fragment
hitting Siberia. Softer than curled steel. Softer than a dip in the drink.

My desire is so dark, it's nauseating. Give me sick motion. Give me
the sensory mismatch of sharp turns and dips. Vertical loops for the gods.

Screams convey six acoustically distinct emotions: anger, fear, joy, passion, pain and sadness. My desire is so dark, it's a disclaimer. "Not Responsible

for Lost Articles." I identify as an analogy about life. No, not a journey! You're mistaking me for someone else. I wait at the centre of the universe.

Buzzkill Clamshell ISO Goddamn

applesaucy / catastrophe, again this marvel
me in 300 characters max: eerie wife
a doomed snow turkey trussed in butcher's twine, flight-
less artifice, buffing spell in a small bottle

muff of malcontent! of mystery! puddlebugged
roadside attraction, melted sugar hips—drizzle
fix for depressed sapphics. i'm the quintessential
squelchy axe wound, weeping mean cream & sludge & slugs
my interests are best described as mercurial
as autonomic $\Longleftrightarrow$ as volatile arousal
if that makes sense? fickle kinks? lunar rot, you know?
i'm looking for other cryptic materials

applesaucy / catastrophe, again this marvel
double stuffed with astonishment. please, stop this app

i want to get off! where are the other kronks? you:
plot twist, an easter egg hidden in the text. you:
put the "fig" in figment, the "ream" in dreamy. you:
must love dogs, oops I mean *god, you must love goddamn
fuckbowls bulljuice errorgasms clownsticks lambslams
fear play too. maybe you want your limestone quarried?
maybe i need my shoal of gold minnows worried?

maybe you want your █████ worshipped? maybe my buzzkill
needs clamshell training? could we bow & down together?
applesaucy / catastrophe, again this marvel

Lez Prophéties

For forty years the rainbow will not be seen.
For forty years it will be seen every day.
—NOSTRADAMUS, *The Prophecies*, translated by Alexis Lykiard

I

To dream of a snake is good luck.
To spit on a fire is bad luck. To spit
on the sacrosanct asshole of the universe
arouses something beyond fate.

II

The prophecies of Nostradamus missed queer
orgasms altogether. Sad astrologer foresaw
disasters and disasters, meanwhile I have learned
to read sweat marks on bicycle seats.

III

Divination by clouds—cumulus means that within
this confusing panoply of beauty and misfortune,
you still matter. Stratus predicts that soon
your ass will be as swollen as aurora gold.

IV

I scry the last sip of water in the glass
left on her bedside table. Her hiss is a kissed mirror.
A dream keyhole through which I enjoy peeping.
Sacred babes slip out of their Orphic eggshells.

V

The two-thousand-year-old dildo on display
at the Roman Vindolanda museum is our inheritance.
The empire once used disembodied phalli to ward off evil.
Fortune is nothing but a cock hatefucking fallacious time.

VI

The footprints bunking up the bathroom tile after I
jerk off under the faucet's gush reveal the future.
Ichnomancy. Our first-born will be the slattern, a chosen one
who will gooch gwank us into a new era of salvation.

VII

Spodomancy is our shared practice, our innate gift.
All queers can predict the future by studying soot and ash.
We know fire. Loss and renewal and loss and renewal
is the original nonnormative life cycle.

VIII

My gag reflex is a gift of grace. The ghost
on my tongue lowers a lifeline to the ghost holed in my throat.
Dark passage. Heaving echo. The weight of fear is a rough haul.
Her cock is the light at the end. We're almost free.

IX

Fae-jack your lover under the full moon. Once charged
and consecrated, turn her splayed legs toward you and read.
The cum sludged on her left thigh will show you your past.
The cum sludged on her right reveals things yet to happen.

X

Spilt sugar means new love is coming.
Spilt wine means thirsty ghosts may have a sip.
Cum spilt on the floor of a filthy bathroom stall
bestows good luck upon everyone at the queer bar.

AMBER DAWN is a writer and creative educator living on the unceded territories of the Musqueam, Squamish, and Tsleil-Waututh First Nations. Her body of work explores queer identity, trauma-informed cultural production, and sex work justice. Her debut novel, *Sub Rosa* (2010), won the Lambda Literary Award for Lesbian Debut Fiction and the Writers' Trust of Canada Dayne Ogilvie Prize. Her memoir, *How Poetry Saved My Life: A Hustler's Memoir* (2013), won the Vancouver Book Award. Her poetry collection *Where the words end and my body begins* (2015) was a finalist for BC and Yukon Book Prizes' Dorothy Livesay Poetry Prize. Her sophomore novel, *Sodom Road Exit* (2018), was a finalist for the Lambda Literary Award for Lesbian Fiction and a Sunburst Award for Excellence in Canadian Literature of the Fantastic. Her collection of long poems, *My Art Is Killing Me and Other Poems* (2020), was a finalist for the Jim Deva Prize for Writing That Provokes.